Learn to Make Decisions

N Chokkan

Learn to Make Decisions
© *New Horizon Media*

First Edition: December 2009
64 Pages
Printed in India.

ISBN 978-81-8493-370-3
Pro-ya-en-67

Prodigy Books
177/103, First Floor, Ambal's Building
Lloyds Road, Royapettah, Chennai 600 014.
Ph: +91-44-4200-9603
Email: support@nhm.in
Website: www.nhm.in

Prodigy Books is an imprint of New Horizon Media Pvt. Ltd.

Contents

The art of decision making

Imagine you are a doctor.

It's a cool profession, right? People come to you with lots of health problems, diseases and you cure them with your magical fingers. Wow!

But let us get closer and watch a real doctor in action. Is it really fun being a doctor?

Not at all. Every minute, doctors face tough situations, and they need to make a decision quick enough, otherwise a life might be in danger. For example, imagine a newborn baby. It's cute, pink in colour, sleeping at one time, but suddenly starts crying and its face becomes red. The baby could be in trouble.

The nurse comes running, 'Doctor, please come, the newborn baby is having some problems.'

The doctor rushes up to the baby, takes a look and is shocked. The baby's body colour has suddenly changed indicating that something really bad is happening.

With a newborn baby, many things can go wrong. It may be a simple change in temperature, skin infection, wrong food intake or a serious problem with the heart, lungs, blood circulation and so on. But the doctor has no time to think about all these for long. He has to make a decision immediately, and act on it as soon as possible, otherwise it may be too late.

Doctors are not magicians. They tend to make good and bad decisions in equal numbers. Then what makes them special? Why they save lives and we don't? The difference is that they have the intelligence and experience to make the right decisions and correct mistakes if any. This comes from years of hard work, learning, and updating their skills on a continuous basis.

Fortunately, not everybody makes such life-threatening decisions on a regular basis. At the same time, everyone, even a small child, makes decisions on a regular basis. So it is important to know the art behind making the right decisions the smart way.

For example, Let us say you want to cross the road and go to the shop on the other side of the road. What do you do? Look to the left side of the road, then to your right, and then left again. You need to make a very important decision – is the road really empty? Should I move on or wait for some more time?

Sometimes, when the road is very wide, you decide to wait till there is absolutely no traffic on the road. If the road is narrower, you may dash across it, even when you see a car coming far away. This is because you have a feeling that you can cross the road before the car comes closer.

This is the art of decision making. Starting from such simple decisions to very complex ones such as — which subjects to choose, which college to attend, which job to select and so on — your life is going to be full of problems that need your attention, and require your decisions on a regular basis.

But how do we really make decisions? Is it a skill we can learn?

Yes, of course. We shall discuss many techniques for decision making in this book, with lots of examples. Feel free to make your own decision as to which tool is to be used in which situation. Now it's time to jump into the decision making pool!

Six companions

Do you have servants at home?

Many people do. Especially when both the parents are working, they need some domestic help to take care of all the cleaning, cooking and other kinds of work. But these servants are available only during certain time of the day, say, 9 a.m. to 6 p.m. After that, they need to go back home to take care of the family, isn't it?

Suppose you are travelling out of your city, you may need help in the new place. In that case you may have to take your servants with you, or hire a new person at the new place. It's a big pain. Wouldn't it be nice if we have a set of servants, who are always with us? Supporting us in everything we do, all the time?

There was a famous English poet named Rudyard Kipling. He had six honest men as his companions, and took them along wherever he went. According to Kipling, these men were not just servants, but very intelligent people who taught him everything he came to know in life.

Who are those special people? Well, they are not really people but six questions which form the basis for all the intelligence in this world:

- What?

- Why?

- When?

- How?

- Where?

- Who?

If you observe carefully, these questions will help us light up any dark situation. Let us take a simple example to explore this concept. You are at the dinner table, and mother says you should eat spinach curry. But you don't feel like having it. Instead of rejecting it outright, try to use few of Kipling's servants. The answers to these questions may reason out why you should eat the spinach.

First... Why Spinach?

It has lot of iron. So it is good for health.

How? When you eat spinach, it enriches your bones with iron, and makes them stronger. Similarly, it helps to improve hemoglobin content in the blood.

Spinach probably looks more attractive now than earlier. Why? Because, we asked the questions, answered them, and got the information.

You are familiar with cartoon characters like Superman, Spiderman, Hulk and many others on the television. But in reality, there is no other super power like information. If you have it on hand, no decision is difficult.

Consider this curious case, which happened in Mumbai a few years back. In a huge factory equipped with the latest machinery for manufacturing cars, thousands of people were also working, non-stop. Suddenly, an important machine broke down, and simply could not be re-started. Due to this, car production was immensely affected. The workers panicked and approached the manager for help. He immediately rushed to the spot and checked a few things on the machine, but it was of no use.

Everyone was worried that no car will roll out of the factory without the machine's functioning. To speed up the repair, they decided to call an expert. The expert mechanic was in Delhi, he had to fly down to Mumbai to look into the problem. Once he arrived at the factory, he took only two minutes to assess the situation, asked a few questions and tightened a few nuts and bolts. Voila! The machine was up and running immediately, as if nothing had gone wrong. The factory manager jumped with joy. He congratulated the expert and asked him for his bill.

'That would be ten thousand rupees,' said the expert.

'My god!' the manager was shocked, 'So much for a five minute job?'

The expert smiled and said, 'All of you had several five minutes on hand but none of you could solve the problem, isn't it?'

'Very true' the manager nodded in approval, and agreed to pay the entire amount to the expert.

This is the difference between doing 'something' and following a structured process for decision making. When you have experience and know what you are doing, where you are going, the chances of success are more. This process of asking six (or more) questions to analyse a situation is called 'data gathering'. It is very important for making decisions in any situation.

As a practical example, consider this small exercise. If you want to go for a movie, how will you decide which theatre to watch the movie in? There are many factors you may have to weigh upon before you make a decision on this; How much money do I have on hand? Where is the theatre? How would I reach there? Can I walk up the distance? Or do I have to travel by bus or taxi? What are the other movie choices I have? Do I like them? Have I already seen them? In my present mood, what kind of movie do I want to see — action, cartoon, humour or something totally new?

When you ask these questions to yourself, you will be able to make a more realistic choice, than blindly selecting a movie and rushing to watch it. In that case, you may get terribly disappointed and return with a heavy heart. Why should you put yourself in such a situation?

In the next chapter, let us learn to make a very simple but extremely important decision. Are you ready?

Say yes or no!

How to say NO

Do you know what a binary is?

It's a pattern recognised by computers, containing a series of 0s and 1s. A computer can represent anything—a word, a picture, an audio file, or a video in binary language. In real life also, we can see binary situations—day and night, up and down, black and white, and of course our favourite, yes and no.

The words yes and no are supposed to be equal in nature. But in reality, one of them weighs on us heavily than the other. Imagine someone is telling you, 'Come, let's play'. Only two answers are possible – yes or no.

It is always easier to say yes because you don't have to really worry about anything. You are basically agreeing to whatever the other person says, so everything will be fine once you say 'yes'. On the other hand, if you have to say no, even though it is also a genuine choice of yours, the disagreement is immediately apparent. What if your best friend asks you for a game? How can you say no? Isn't it insulting?

The problem is that the world sees 'no' as a negative answer, and the person who says it is considered a spoilsport, odd man out, or a rotten potato. But what is the reality? As we saw earlier, saying yes pleases everyone. But is that a right choice?

Let us say we are in the middle of an examination. The guy sitting next to you is asking you: 'Psst, please help me, tell me the answer for question number 8, will you?'

Now it is very easy to say 'yes'. After all, you want to help your friend, don't you?

Moreover, if you say 'no' it might hurt the other person. After the exam is over, he may stop talking to you, or worse, his friends may come and beat you up for not helping their friend in the examination.

But if you say 'yes' instead of 'no' because you are afraid of the consequences it might hurt you in the long run. If you decide to help your friend by allowing him to copy your exam papers, a vigilant teacher may throw both of you out of the exam hall. So, saying 'yes' or agreeing to others may look like an easy solution. But in the long run, it is not advisable to say 'yes' when you don't want to.

This doesn't mean 'yes' is a bad answer or 'no' is a good answer. It all depends on the situation and you should never feel bad about saying 'no' when that is the best decision for that scenario. But this is not easy. The world looks at those who say 'no' with a wrong attitude. Just look at your parents - when they ask you to do some work, they expect you to say 'yes' and won't take 'nos' for an answer. But if there is a good reason for you to say 'no,' you shouldn't hesitate or say 'yes', just because that's the answer they want to hear from you.

For example, tomorrow there is an exam, and your father calls you for a quick game of chess. Now you may say 'No dad, I need to study'.

Suddenly, 'no' has become a good, acceptable answer. How?

Simple. You padded it up with a reason. That's all!

Communication experts call it 'sugarcoating'. You are giving a bad medicine, but coating it with enough sweetness so that it doesn't hurt when the other person swallows it. So, your 'no's need sugarcoating. How can we do it? First of all, whether you say 'yes' or 'no' there should be reason behind whatever you are saying or doing. That helps us put things in perspective.

Mrs. and Mr. Purva are planning to go to a family friend's wedding. Their only daughter Pooja also wants to join them. But the marriage hall is far away. Travelling all the way there and returning will be very tiring for Pooja.

She won't be able to finish her homework on time, or get ready for school the next day.

Mrs. Purva tries to explain all these to her daughter, but Pooja is very adamant. 'I too want to go,' she cries.

Now, her father takes a different approach. He says, 'Dear, day after tomorrow is a Saturday and there is a children's fair arranged in the city hall, I will take you to the programme, if you agree to stay at home tonight, okay?'

Aha, that's a deal. Pooja agrees immediately!

This is the magic of sugarcoating. Even when the answer 'no' is bitter, people don't see it that way. But isn't that cheating? Not at all. Both yes and no are perfectly valid answers to a problem. We are only trying to explain this to others, by providing reasons behind our 'no's.

At one end, we have 'yes' and at the other end it is 'no'. Is there a choice in between? Of course, it's called 'Let's see'. It is a very famous response used by many people around the world. Consider what happens in a court. When there is a case between two people, the judge listens to the arguments of both parties and tries to make a decision. It's not easy. He may have to think about so many things, consider various angles, refer to earlier cases, discuss with a few experts if required, and finally arrive at a conclusion. All these take time.

So, he decides to 'reserve' his judgment. In other words, he is buying more time to think about the problem and arrive at an optimal solution. We can also use this 'judgment reserved' technique effectively in many situations. How? Experts say we need to buy time for making any decision. Unless and until it's a medical emergency, or the building is on fire, and people can't afford to wait.

Remember, we are not buying time to sit and relax. Time has to be effectively used for collecting the background information, other facts about the problem in hand, and for considering an optimal response or solution. Another reason is, when you are in a hurry, we tend to move away from rational thinking and make an emotional decision. On the other hand, when you take a break and think about it slowly and carefully, logical brain takes over.

Observe what chess players do. Just because there are so many coins and boxes on the table, they don't move them rapidly, or do whatever comes to their mind first. They stop and think about various movements, how their opponents may react to them, and finally make their choice. We can follow the same in any situation – take a deep breath, collect as much information about the problem as possible, analyze them effectively and finally say 'yes' or 'no' without worrying about what others may think about it!

Understand the problem

Have you seen a world map? It's huge. But when you observe closely, you can clearly see the countries and important cities marked with precision. We may not appreciate the value of it now, but when we travel, it's of good use. Can you draw a similar map of your house or of your school?

Sure. But why? The house is not very big. When compared to that, the school is bigger, but you know both these places very well. A map won't be necessary. True, but imagine a friend of yours coming to visit you. Won't such a map be useful for them to get to the place they want quickly?

Decision making also gives us a similar challenge, the need for a map. Assume that problem is the source and solution or decision is the destination — the journey from the source to the destination is very important. This is where maps can help us a lot.

There are various maps that help us travel between the problem and the corresponding solution effectively, without losing our way in between. Let us explore one of them in detail.

This particular map contains 10 steps or landmarks. They are:

1. Define the problem and the expected solution

2. Collect data

3. List solution possibilities

4. Weigh possibilities

5. Get expert help

6. Filter mismatches

7. Decide on a solution

8. Stay focused on the agreed solution

9. Execute

10. Monitor/control/rework

Now let us get started, from the first step in this map, towards our optimal solution. Everything starts with defining the problem clearly. Without that, the solution won't be realistic or complete. Looks so simple — after all, we know our problem, isn't it?

The truth is, no. Many times people look for solutions without even clearly knowing or stating what the problem is. Similarly, people also don't know what is the solution expected out of a situation. They simply don't like the present uneasiness and want to get rid of it. But they don't really know where they want to be, or how they want to feel when the problem disappears.

For example, a student who scores very low marks in every mathematics exam may state his problem like this: 'I am not good at math. That's the issue I want to solve.'

Okay, but how? He has to define the expected solution also. At this point, he may not know how he is going to achieve the expected outcome. But it doesn't matter - all we need is, clearly state where you want to be: 'I want to score at least 85% in every exam next year, including the final exam.'

Now things are clearer, we will be able to progress towards this goal with confidence. The second step is to collect data. Any problem looks very big when we look at it from outside. But if you get closer, and get on to the details, you can see the solutions emerging from it.

Another angle is, when we don't know the minute details about the problem we are facing, we tend to overestimate the level of issue on hand, which creates panic and reduces the motivation to succeed. To avoid such situations, we need to collect as much information as possible about the problem on hand. The more we get to know, the better.

Going back to our mathematics example, we may have to collect information such as: what are the topics under Math that the student lacks knowledge, why, what methods he has adopted, and why they are failing, and what strategy is being adopted by other children of his age.

When we collect such data, the problem which looked like a jigsaw puzzle, slowly starts to make sense. We are able to see some patterns emerging out of the earlier madness, and use them to our benefit. Now, we know the problem in detail. We have a fair understanding of how this should be solved. The subsequent steps are going to take us towards this decision, on a fast track.

Think out-of-the-box

What is 2 + 2? When your teacher gives you a Maths problem like this, there can only be one solution to it. The answer is the same for a five year old as well as a great scientist — 4. On the other hand, if the teacher asks you a different question, 'When you grow up, what do you want to be?' This is called an 'open ended question' because there can be hundreds, thousands and even millions of answers to this simple question.

Similarly, when there is a problem on hand, you may treat it as open ended question or close your mind to it. This will determine 'how many' different solutions you get for that. Is it really important? Yes. It is important to know all possible choices you have on hand before you make a decision.

Imagine that you don't want to eat oily food in the morning. And your mother has made some dosas and vadas for breakfast. What will you do? There are no options, right? Eat the oily food and run to the school.

Instead, if you open the refrigerator and find fresh apples, it is another choice you have, which you didn't try to explore. A problem can also have more than one or two solutions. Several times, we don't see it immediately and end up making the most obvious decisions, and regretting it later.

To avoid this, we need to start considering any problem as an open ended question, think out-of-the-box and arrive at solutions which you normally don't think of. Consider this case – your cousin is coming home for the weekend, but you are down with flu. What can you do? The obvious choices are:

1. Forget the flu, play with him and have fun, the fever might subside on its own.

2. Say sorry and remain in bed.

Imagine something beyond these two choices and explore what else is possible in such a situation. This needs a different thought process, which is called "Lateral thinking." There are many games which you can play even while you are down with fever in bed — monopoly, video games, watching movies and so on. On any other day, you may not consider these as fun, but now, since you are down with fever and your cousin is also visiting you, you start thinking of unusual ways to find a third solution — other than the two we discovered earlier.

In fact, if you apply your mind to it, you may find many other solutions to the same problem. This is the important third step in decision making. A word of caution though: When you are imagining decision solutions, don't think about what will work, what won't, and reject an idea because of that. We can worry about those later. For the moment, it is important for us to pile up as many solutions as possible.

When you start imagining things even the usual bottlenecks and showstoppers will slowly vanish. When you have an option as a possible solution, you start thinking about how to make it happen. On the other hand, if you worry about what will work even before you consider the idea seriously, you are doing damage to your own thinking process. It blocks your thinking and makes you reject something useful at a very early stage.

Here goes a story of a young man who was very poor. He couldn't support his family and was desperately crying for help. One day, god appeared in front of him and asked, 'What do you want?'

He was thrilled to see God in front of him, and was dumbstruck. After lot of thinking, he said, 'God, please give me some job to support my family members.'

God agreed and gave him a forest full of sandalwood trees. 'I hope you can live happily selling these?'

'Oh yes, Thank you Lord.'

God vanished, and the young man went home happily.

Next day, he started cutting all the sandalwood trees on his own forest area and took them to the market. He sold them for 100 rupees and returned with lots of food, toys and clothes. This continued for the next few days and finally, it was all over. The forest was empty.

The young man started crying again, 'Oh God, I have lost everything. What will I do now?'

God appeared out of nowhere and asked, 'What happened? Why are you crying?'

'Lord, I sold all the sandalwood you gave and spent the money. Now I am poor again.'

God was shocked, 'Those sandalwood trees were enough to last a few generations. How can you clean them up in just three months? Even if you do, you should be very rich by now.'

He said, 'No God, I sold them to merchants for burning wood as fuel, and they paid me very little.'

God smiled and said, 'Oh no, sandalwood is very valuable and you should have sold them to people who make articles out of them. They would have paid you handsomely.'

The man was very upset. But there is no point thinking about it now, it is too late. This is the value of making choices. When you think inside a box, you can achieve very little. Just go out of it, think of all other things you have been ignoring, or refusing to see all these days, and sky is the limit for you.

But having too many choices is also a problem. How do we choose one among them? Don't worry; there are many solutions for this too. We shall discuss one of them in the next chapter, as our fourth step in decision making.

Weigh your choices

Ah, I am very hungry; can I get something to eat? Yes. But before that, you must wash your hands.

Why? What will happen if we don't wash our hands and dig into the food directly?

There are millions of germs in our hands, which may find their way into our body through the mouth. Then they will attack our organs and cause illnesses. To avoid this, we must wash our hands before any meal.

But, where are the germs? I don't see them! True. Because the germs are so tiny, we need a microscope to see them. A microscope magnifies the germs and makes them appear bigger, thus becoming visible to our eyes.

Like the microscope, there is a special tool that helps us to analyse various solution choices, and pick the best one out. This is the fourth step in decision making where we weigh our choices and decide which one will fit the current scenario.

The name of this amazing tool is SWOT. It means:

- S – Strengths
- W – Weaknesses
- O – Opportunities
- T – Threats

Let us take a simple example and explore how SWOT works. Similarly, you can imagine any problem, its solutions and analyze them using this tool. Today is a holiday and you are not able to decide what to do—should you stay at home and watch television, or go out and play?

Choice 1 – Staying at home and watching television. Put it under the SWOT tool for analysis: First, what are the strengths of this solution? Being at home the whole day means mother will be making you some special sweets and snacks. Those yummy dishes will make the holiday even more enjoyable.

But there is a flip side to this, staying at home makes you feel very lonely. All your friends will be playing in the ground and having lots of fun, but you will be all alone in front of the television. This is the weakness of this solution. Are there any opportunities? Yes. As we don't move away from home, we can decide how long to watch television, and catch-up on home work in between. When dad comes home, you can ask him to take you out and it will be lot more fun.

Finally, the threats. For your mother, holidays are for completing chores around the house. She has a big list, which you are supposed to take care of. Completing all the work on the list will take two full days and there won't be any holiday left for you to enjoy.

Similarly, take choice 2 and do a SWOT analysis. Then it becomes easy for you to weigh the strengths, weaknesses, opportunities, and threats presented by each choice. Pick the one which gives you the maximum benefit. For your practice, here are some situations and possible solutions. Do your SWOT analysis and decide upon what might be the best choice.

- It's a rainy day, you are at school, and your parents won't be here for the next one hour.
- You are visiting your aunt's village, and there is no television in their home. How can you spend the next 4 days there?
- Tomorrow you have a class test, and you need to read a lot for that. But now you are feeling very sleepy, should you sleep now and wake-up early morning tomorrow?
- Your birthday party is arranged in a pompous hotel but there are more guests than expected. Mother and father are worried, what can you do to help them out?

SWOT analysis is very powerful for weighing options. To make it even better, you can use 'scores'.

When you write an examination, your teacher assigns you a score, right? Similarly, when you read choices and do analysis, you can calculate the scores of each one of them to speed up your decision making process. If a problem has five possible solutions and their scores are 12, 15, 12, 14 and 16, which one will you choose?

Easy — the solution with the highest score is the best choice, naturally. But how will we assign scores to each solution? Is there a magic formula for this too? You bet. There are not one but many popular techniques to make this happen. One of them is PM.

You guessed it right! PM is the short form of a very useful magic formula. PM stands for:

- P – Plus
- M – Minus

The PM technique is similar to SWOT. But this time round, we will be assigning numeric values to all the elements in the analysis to calculate the final score. Imagine you are invited for a buffet breakfast in a hotel. You can either have a simple sandwich, juice or a bowl of corn flakes with hot milk. Let us do PM analysis on these two choices and decide on the best option.

Sandwich and juice: What are the plus points and minus points in having this? The vegetables in the sandwich are fresh, the bread contains the fibre you need and the juice is also freshly squeezed, giving you nutrients and energy. On the minus side, sandwich has a bland taste which you don't enjoy, and juice looks like it's too watered down.

So, plus 3, minus 2 — the score for this solution is '1'.

Here goes the second option: A bowl of corn flakes with hot milk. Do the same PM analysis.

Plus: Corn flakes are fortified with all the required nutrients. It is of chocolate flavour which you love, and mother says milk is very good for your health. Moreover, you like the taste of corn flakes and hot milk.

Minus: Food is not fresh… and there seems to be no other minus point in it. So the score is Plus 4, Minus 2 that equals '2'. After this analysis, it is very easy for us to make a choice between decision 1 (sandwich and juice) and decision 2 (corn flakes with hot milk). As the second decision has a higher score, we opt for that.

This doesn't mean that sandwiches are bad. It is just an example to teach us how to make a decision based on PM scores. When you have one or more choices, using PM technique is not really necessary. You can make a choice by just making an apple to apple comparison between the available options.

On the other hand, when there are more than 2 choices, it is always preferred to make a score-based comparison (like PM analysis) and make an analytical choice!

Getting expert opinion

What is the difference between cricket and tennis? Quite obvious - tennis is an individual sport whereas cricket is a team sport. Many people have to play together and do their job well as a team to win a match. But that doesn't mean a tennis player becomes a champion with his or her own efforts. They have a coach, nutritionist and other support personnel, who help the player win.

In either case, a winning team is the one that makes the best use of its experts. This brings a whole new synergy on to the table, which is absent when individuals play on their own. In a cricket team, a wicket keeper is an expert in his field of play. And if that expertise is missing, the team won't be able to perform better. At the same time, without others' help, a wicket keeper also cannot achieve much.

The reason we are bringing this into equation, step 5 in decision making is getting expert help, as necessary.

Learn to Make Decisions

Till now, we have seen lots of examples on decision making. In almost all of them, you were alone in arriving at a decision or a set of choices. This is easy, as long as you know the situation and have the required skill sets to think of a solution. What if you don't have those? That's when experts come into the picture.

You want to buy a bicycle, for which you are planning to save your pocket money. But where can you keep it? At home, in a small box? Or give it to your mother for safekeeping? Or, put it in a bank account? The choice becomes difficult for you because you are not an expert in this. So, you seek help from someone who is an expert. You may ask your father: 'Dad, I've been thinking about this and these are the choices I could think of, what do you suggest?'

By asking an expert, you are achieving two things. #1, you bring fresh energy into your team (which was non-existent till now) and #2, this additional pair of eyes may pin down obvious mistakes, if any, in what you have been doing so far. This will most likely increase your productivity.

Dad says, 'Good job son, these are fantastic choices, but have you thought about this? If you save money like this, it will take you four years before you can afford a bicycle.'

Oops. You never thought of that! What can you do now? There's no need for you to panic. You have an expert in your team. Whenever there is a problem, it is most likely that the expert knows the solution, or at least a part of it. So make use of the expertise!

'Dad, that's a very difficult question, I am not sure how to decide on this.'

'May be, in addition to your pocket money, you should also save the cash you get from me, your mother and other relatives for your birthday?'

'But nobody gives me cash. Everyone gives me some gift or the other.'

'That was the case earlier. Now that we know you are saving for the bicycle, we will be glad to help in your efforts. Don't worry!'

'So, if I save that money also, can I buy a bicycle in 6 months?'

'May be, let us do the calculation and decide on the strategy.'

Now you can clearly see the difference between making a decision all alone and getting expert help. It definitely adds value to the whole process.

However, one thing you need to remember is that experts are not always available. Even if they are around, they may be busy, or may not able to help you for some reason or the other. So you shouldn't become too dependent on them. After all, it's your decision, not theirs.

Whenever you get help from experts, observe what they do, and ask questions when you are not able to understand something. Don't worry if their answer is cryptic and confusing, ask more and more questions and try to capture as much information as possible. This will not only make you an expert but also helps you understand the decision making process. Next time there is a similar problem, you will be able to do a lot more homework before you approach an expert. This also gives them a feeling that you are trying hard, and they will support you wholeheartedly.

Once you have got expert help and validated (or improved on) your decision ideas, the sixth step is removing the mismatches. But before that, what are mismatches? There are certain ideas which will look good on paper. But when you start implementing them, they will fail for some reason or other. You should learn to see such mismatches well in advance.

Another point to remember is that these mismatches are specific to each individual. One idea which fits me very well may turn out to be a mismatch for you. Sometimes, they depend on the situation. A decision may be wise now, not tomorrow, or next month. So, you should learn to visualise the solution in your mind and remove the mismatches well in advance, based on your personal choices, situation, and any other factors that may affect your decision.

Take for example, Sunder. He is very fat; everyone calls him names and teases him. He decides to reduce his weight by 5 kilograms. There are many decisions he can make based on this goal. One of them may be, running 3 kilometres in the morning and 4 in the evening. It's a nice idea and it sure will work. But unfortunately, his school starts at 8:30 in the morning and he has to catch the school bus by 7:45 a.m. This leaves him with very little time to run, at least in the mornings. Hence, he will have to think of some other alternatives like diet control or afternoon exercises.

On the other hand, if Sunder's school is nearby, he can just walk to school starting at 8:15 a.m. This will give him some time in the morning, to run a few kilometres. In fact, he can even speed walk to the school making the best use of the time available. Or use the school ground for running once he reaches school.

The point is to filter mismatches as early as possible. If we don't, we will be attempting at something useless and will realise it late. Not only is time wasted, you also tend to lose motivation for continuing further. The next (seventh) step in decision making is the most important one. Using all the data collected, analysis performed, expert help, and filtering the mismatches, we are going to actually 'decide'. This means we are picking one choice from many.

At this juncture arises a curious question: should I go for only one choice? Or can I try multiple choices? Usually, it is preferred and also recommended that people go forward with a single focus. This will help direct all your energy in the same direction, and distractions are avoided. You will be able to perform better and measure your progress. Some people prefer to call this 'Decision A' or 'Plan A'. This means, there should be a 'Plan B' also. Not always.

You have to understand that however good your 'Plan A' is, there is no assurance that it will always succeed. So many things can go wrong, which you may or may not expect in advance. To summarise, there is nothing wrong in keeping a 'Plan B' ready at the back of your head, just in case 'Plan A' fails.

Keep a primary decision and a secondary decision on hand. But focus all your energies only on the primary decision. In case something goes wrong, don't panic, and just go with the second decision. Again, visualisation is very important. Every decision we make should be implemented in a way that would make it work, and the consequences should be visualised well in advance. The more you visualise the better focussed your energies will be.

Whenever you plan for a short trip, just observe what your parents do. They will be thinking of the time available on hand and various other factors during the planning of the same trip, in multiple ways!

It makes a lot of sense because so many things can go wrong, and being extra cautious definitely helps!

The right choice

There is a famous proverb in English: 'Those who fail to plan are planning to fail'.

But what does decision making have to do with planning? Aren't they two different things? True. But they are so inter-twined that you can't do one without the other. This is a very important point that decision makers ought to realise. That's why the last three steps in decision making are important: talking about careful execution, monitoring and rework, if necessary.

Do you have a car at home? Or a bike? Observe its control panel. What are the items that you see? Usually any powered vehicle will have a speedometer. There may be additional controls to indicate how much fuel is there in the tank, water level, temperature control, distance travelled and so on. When you look inside the cockpit of an aeroplane, the control panel is full of monitors and meters.

The primary reason behind having all these is to monitor. Even though the destination has been decided upon, it is very important for us to monitor how we are doing and compare it with the original plan. If there are some mismatches, we need to take the necessary corrective measures to stay right on track.

Suppose you are on a long journey with a perfect plan. But half way through, your petrol tank becomes empty and you are stranded on the road. You could have easily avoided this, had you checked the petrol level indicator continuously. Whenever it dips down to dangerously low levels, you just have to find the nearest fuel station and fill it up.

This technique can be applied to monitoring and taking corrective actions for any decision or solution. It increases and ensures the possibility of success in implementing our decisions. Let us go back to the bicycle example in our previous chapter. With the help of an expert, you have finalised how you want to save for the bicycle and started saving.

Your target is to buy a bicycle by end of this year. If you wait that long, you may end up disappointed due to paucity of funds. To be on the safer side, it is advisable for you to look into your savings account on a regular basis. You may have to regularly count how much you have already saved, how much more to go and plan alternative strategies, if necessary.

If your aim is to save 1000 rupees in one year, and you have saved 100 rupees in two months, by the end of the year, you may have just 600 rupees, well below your target. So you may think why you have saved less than your expectations. Is there any other way to do some additional work and earn money? How can you come back on track before next month's review?

Alternatively, within the same two months, if you could save 200 rupees, you needn't worry. As long as you continue the same way, you should reach your target well ahead of time. This kind of analysis is very important in effective implementation of any decision. The process of closely monitoring the progress of any task on a regular basis is called 'review'.

Usually, the review can be done by you, against the originally stated goals. But it is always advisable to get help from someone else, so that they don't overlook your performance. Others will be more critical and help you come back on track easily.

Remember, the others are out there to help you. If they point out some mistakes and suggest corrective actions, don't take them personally. Accept them wholeheartedly and implement them as much as possible. It's for the greater good of everyone. Finally, once the execution process is completed, we need to do a thorough analysis of what we did. This process is called 'post-mortem'.

Review and post-mortem are somewhat similar. The only difference is that a review is done on a regular basis during the implementation of the decision, whereas post-mortem is done after the execution is over. Here we calculate the effectiveness of the implementation by comparing the original goals with the actual results.

You wanted to save 1000 rupees in 12 months, but you have saved 980 rupees. You are 98% effective in reaching your target.

On the other hand, if you had saved the same 1000 rupees in 10 months, your execution worked more efficiently than the original plan; you can pat yourself on the back! The most important lesson is to learn from your mistakes and remember them when making your next decision. That's real progress!

This too shall pass

Have you heard about the Wright Brothers? They are the famous people who invented aeroplanes. They were the ones who succeeded in inventing a flying machine. Before them, many others tried, but failed. Inventing a plane is not child's play. If you fail, it is almost the end of your life, there is no second chance. It's very scary.

Still, Wright Brothers didn't lose hope. Both were willing to risk their lives on this mission. This is what made them succeed in inventing an aeroplane. Similarly, there are some real life problems that are assumed to be impossible. In such scenarios, people think no decision can be taken, and that blocks their thought process.

When Albert Einstein started doing his science experiments, experts across the world believed time is absolute. This belief was prevalent for centuries, and nobody dared to think beyond this. Because of this, many problems were considered impossible, and scientists gave up hope on solving them.

However, Einstein didn't accept this assumption. He felt no situation is hopeless, and no rules are rigid. He tried to break the common belief that time is absolute, and this led him to various discoveries. This is a very important lesson in decision making. Sometimes, when you are dealing with a problem, however hard you may think, you draw a blank, and no decision seems to be final, and it looks like an impossible situation.

There is nothing that is impossible. As the famous proverb goes, even the word can be changed to I'm Possible. So, when you are not able to find any solution to a particular problem, remember this magic phrase. It contains only four words but is very powerful:

This too shall pass

It sounds very simple and obvious. But at the same time it is a very complex and realistic saying, applicable for anyone and everyone. Years ago, there was a king who was given this formula. He laughed at it and said, 'It's stupid.' His minister smiled and said, 'Oh king, please believe me. Just keep this lesson in your mind, and follow this everyday. You will definitely see the difference, and I promise it will change your life some day.'

The king agreed. He wrote it down on a piece of parchment and kept it in his royal crown. A few days later, his enemies attacked him and the king had to flee.

When he was in a jungle, with nobody to help him, no food to eat, and all by himself, he felt distressed. The situation looked impossible, and he couldn't decide what to do next. When he casually removed his royal crown, he saw the parchment. It said "This too shall pass".

Now, the statement made sense to the king. It brought his energy back. He gathered supporters, planned an attack and won his kingdom back. When the king came back to power, the people were very happy. They organised huge celebrations, sang songs and danced in praise of their emperor.

Seeing all these, the king felt very happy. But the parchment inside his royal crown reminded him, this too shall pass, and he remained grounded forever.

This story is a perfect example for making impossible decisions. The fact is, if you apply your mind over an issue, there is nothing impossible. All you need is the right attitude and tireless efforts. So, what should we do when we are not able to decide on anything?

First, we need to make sure we have dotted all the 'i's and crossed all the 't's. This means we have to check whether we have considered all the possibilities? It is very easy to say 'yes' to this question. But that's pure escapism. You can never be sure if all possible decisions are well analysed.

In the example of the Wright Brothers, they had tried almost everything; still they couldn't invent a successful aeroplane. That's what got them thinking. Let's also go beyond that 'almost everything' and try more. We will question all our assumptions, beliefs, prejudices, and look from different angles which nobody else has done.

The Wright Brothers finally arrived at the solution. They perfected the art of balancing and the flying machine; it was the first successful flight ever. As they say in a famous advertisement, impossible is nothing, let's just go beyond that!

The 80:20 rule

Tomorrow, there is a cricket match in school. All the boys are very excited. They want to go to the venue and cheer their school team. But their cricket coach doesn't like it. He strictly said, 'No, tomorrow all of you have to come here and practice the whole day.'

'But sir, it's not an ordinary match. Our school team is playing, and we should be there to support them.'

'I said No,' the coach said firmly. He was not ready to change his mind. The boys were very upset, they returned home worried. One of them said, 'Hey, the coach probably was not very serious about it? May be he wouldn't mind if we skip the practice.'

The others agreed: 'You are right. Let us skip the practice session and watch the game, after all, our school team is playing.' So, the next day they all went to the ground and watched the match. They had lots of fun. But when they returned for cricket practice in the evening, the coach was very angry. He shouted at them, 'What did I say yesterday? How can you go to the match when I had given clear instructions to you, to come here and practice?'

The boys stood silently. All of them hung their heads in shame. The coach picked one boy in particular: 'I don't care about the others; but you are a very talented young boy, and you shouldn't have done this.'

'There are many people out there who will watch cricket. But only a few can play. You have that talent. If you don't respect and nourish it, you will never get anywhere in your cricket career, do you understand?'

The boy understood these words very well, and started following it religiously. He went on to become one of the best cricketers India has ever produced – Sachin Ramesh Tendulkar!

The message given by Sachin's coach Ramakant Achrekar is actually a very famous management theory. It's called the '80:20' rule. Vilfredo Pareto, an Italian expert created this theory. In his honour, it is also called "Pareto's principle". Later, it was refined and made more popular by an American, Dr. Joseph M Juran.

What does the 80:20 Rule say?

In this world, 80% of the things are affected only by 20% of the effort.

Not clear? With an example, you will understand it better. In a day, assume you have 10 works to finish. You have 10 hours to complete all these. Now, how much time you should spend on each one of these tasks?

10 hours/10 tasks = 1 hour each. Right?

Wrong!

Having ten tasks doesn't mean all of them are equally important, or all of them need the same kind of effort. Some of them may be very simple and may get over in 2 minutes, and a few others may drag on for hours. So, what do we do? How can we prioritise and effectively spend time on each task?

This is where Pareto's principle helps us - 80% of the time we have will be normally spent on 20% of the work. In other words, completing that 20% work is the most difficult and important part, once you do it, the rest fall in place, automatically.

You can see practical uses for the 80:20 Principle everywhere:

- A city may have 100 people, and 100 crore rupees of wealth. In that case, 80 crores of this money will be with 20 people only, the other 80 will be sharing the balance 20 crores.

- In your school, most (80%) of the cleaning work is done by just 20% of the students. Others just escape, somehow!

- A company may earn millions of dollars, but most (80%) of this revenue comes from few (20%) customers.

How can we make use of this in decision making?

Let us say, you have multiple problems on hand, and are not able to pick one of them. Now 80:20 Rule comes handy – you can pick one or two problems (20%) which makes a maximum (80%) impact on the overall situation. Similarly, when you follow the regular decision making procedures and arrive at a number of solutions, you may pick one among those by using the same principle. Just observe this: implementation of which solution gives the maximum impact, with minimum effort.

To cite another example, suppose you have to take your Mathematics examination tomorrow morning. But you haven't completed the required preparation for that. And the time available to you is just 8 hours. How can you be fully prepared for the exam within this limited time?

Look up the total number of lessons you have to study, say five. To read and understand them thoroughly, it would take at least two days. Even if you just skim through the lessons and memorise the concepts in general, you will need one day. But there is no time now. So, you decide to just go through the important formulas in each lesson and use it as your preparation. This is the maximum you can do in the available 8 hours.

The decision you made in the available time was on what lessons to study, to get maximum impact—marks. This is exactly what the 80:20 Principle is about. All of us use it unknowingly, everyday. If you start using it consciously in your decision making process, the results will be very rewarding!

The thinking hats

How many caps or hats do you have at home? One, two… a maximum of four or five. You tend to wear them once in a while during special occasions — when you go out on a sunny day, visit a farm, go for a picnic or a cricket match. For a change, let us wear those fantastic hats indoors. They are going to help us in our decision making process. Edward de Bono, a very famous management expert, has introduced a unique concept called 'Six Thinking Hats'. This is used widely by hundreds of organisations and thousands of individuals in improving their thinking and decision making.

The best part is that the hats are of six wonderful colours. When you wear them, you will look different and think different. Those six colours are:

- White hat
- Red Hat
- Black Hat

- Yellow Hat

- Green Hat

- Blue Hat

Well, you know how to wear a hat. But when you wear one, how should you behave? What is its use?

First of all, we shall start with the white hat. It is also called the Information Hat. When you are wearing the white hat, you should only think about the information on hand. Everything you talk about should have a proof; otherwise you better don't mention it.

Assume you are trying to make a decision on which dress to wear for school. When you have your white hat on, you should only think about information such as: What day is it? On this day are there any restrictions on the colour of dress to be worn to school? What dress did I wear yesterday?

But what if you feel like wearing a particular dress today? As you don't have any information to support this feeling, you shouldn't talk about it when wearing the white hat. Wait till you get your red hat on. Red stands for emotions. When you wear this special hat, you don't have to bother about information. Just speak out what is on your mind. There is no need to prove anything to anyone with evidence or statistics. Isn't it fun?

The red hat is extremely useful in getting your feelings out. Sometimes (especially when wearing a white hat), you tend to hesitate to express what is on your mind. It may be right, and may help in your decision making process. So red hat makes you say it, without worrying about anything else.

When you see someone, you immediately say, "Hey, I like this fellow" or "Gee, I hate him/her". There are no reasons for this, you just feel that way, it is important that we capture it during the decision making process. Red hat is your friend to make this happen.

The third is the black hat. As you would have guessed, we are going to talk about negative things here. In fact, only negative things. When you are thinking of an idea, sometimes you get over excited and forget about the misgivings in your thought process. In such scenarios, 'black hat' thinking really helps.

Black hat is nothing but a pessimistic view of the world around you – What if something goes wrong? What if my assumptions are incorrect? In such an event, what is my alternative 'Plan B'?

Remember, Black hat thinking has to be restricted to only when you are wearing this particular hat. Once you take it off, forget your pessimistic approach and start seeing things in a balanced view. Otherwise, you tend to become over-cautious and restrict your thought process, ideas, and everything else.

Don't worry. There is another hat which can help us wipe out the black hat thinking. It's called a yellow hat. While a black hat promotes negative thinking, a yellow hat is for positive thinking. When you wear this, forget all negative things about the decision you are making, think of only positive, in fact over positive things. Imagine what will happen if everything went as planned, and the benefits you will reap out of it.

Yellow hat thinking is good for our health and mind. Being positive about everything and having an optimistic approach to life will expand your thinking horizons and help in everything you do.

Okay. Till now we have discussed all about information (White hat), emotions (Red hat), negatives (Black hat) and positives (Yellow hat). So what's next? In this process, did we miss something? What if we forgot to think about something? Is there a way to find it and bring it to the table? We may need a special hat for this.

Yes. It's called a Green hat!

Green represents grass, trees, forests and everything belonging to Nature. This indicates the creativity with which we can invent new ideas. When you are making decisions, we tend to get into some imaginary boundaries and start thinking within them. When you are wearing a green hat, you should forget about any such restrictions and think afresh and out-of-the-box. Don't worry about the consequences though. Just think something new, and that's it.

When you are thinking of a story to write as homework, it is always easy to write one that someone has told you or you have read in a book. You can make some changes and write it in your own style. It is not so when you are wearing a green hat. You need to think of an all-new story, without worrying about what people will say, or how the story will take shape.

Such creativity brings many new ideas to the decision making process, and is a very valuable tool. In schools, colleges, offices, factories, research facilities and other such places, creative thinkers are respected a lot. Don't you want to be one of them?

Now we come to the last piece of our puzzle, which is the most important one – the blue hat.

When you are participating in a classroom discussion, just observe what your teacher does. She won't be participating in the debate actively. But at the same time, whenever things go out of control, she jumps in and tries to sort out matters by moderating the discussions, making sure that everyone gets a fair chance to talk.

This is exactly what a blue hat thinker does. Because we have five other hats, various kinds of thoughts will be bubbling in your mind. Information from the white hat will compete with the red hat emotions, black negatives will fight with yellow positives and green hat ideas will try to overpower everything else.

So, at the end of such a thinking hat exercise, it is very important that you wear a blue hat and summarise things. If possible, document your thought process and use it as a reference to make the actual decision.

"The six thinking hats" concept is used by students, college-goers, executives, politicians, scientists and many more. They provide an organised framework for thinking and decision making, and improve your productivity.

So, keep those hats handy, always!

Step by step

There are so many buildings around the city, and around the world. It amazes me how they built all these wonderful structures? The answer is very obvious. Any great building has to be constructed brick by brick. There is no other option.

When you look at a chess board, the game looks very complex. So many squares, Kings, Queens, Pawns, Knights, Bishops and many other pieces, and so many rules. You may wonder how you will play the game. Stop worrying. Don't think about all those pieces on the board. Just focus on one move at a time, and you will be fine. In fact, any big journey can be broken into a series of steps. As long as you do one step well, you can focus on the next and so on. No destination is far off or difficult when you follow this approach.

The same can be applied to decision making as well. When there is a problem that seems very complex, simply break them into smaller problems and start finding solutions. Decisions for each one of them will come easily.

In a superfast express running towards Mumbai, all the compartments were very crowded and many people had to travel standing, because all the seats were full. Suddenly, a women cried, 'Oh no, someone stop the train. Please.'

Other people around her asked her with concern, 'What happened? Why do you want to stop the train?'

She said, 'My chain has fallen down.'

'Where?'

'I don't know. It fell down a few minutes back. It's a very costly golden chain.'

Everyone started talking, discussed various strategies, some called for the officials; many others shared their own experiences of having lost jewels, money and other things on a train. Amid this chaos, the woman was still crying. There was one person in the same compartment, who was very silent, calm and composed. He looked out of the window and was very focused on whatever he was trying to see.

Other people who saw this got upset, and they started criticising that person: 'Poor lady, she has lost her golden chain and is crying. But this man doesn't care. May be his heart is made of stone?'

Even after such an insult, that person didn't open his mouth. He was still concentrating on something outside the compartment. After a few minutes, some officials came and stopped the train. They asked the woman where exactly her chain fell.

She said, 'I don't know really. How am I supposed to know?'

The gentleman near the window spoke for the first time: 'I know where the chain fell.'

'But how?'

'Till now, I was counting the electric posts outside, since the chain fell. I could see 484 such posts, you just need to go back that many posts and you will find her chain there.'

Everyone applauded him. They all understood how important it is to find a solution than worry about the complexity of the problem. When you look from outside, the problem of a lost chain in a running train looks very complex. But when you break the same, it is just a matter of finding a way of knowing where it fell, and that gentleman found a nice way to calculate it and executed it to perfection, and he won.

In any mystery story, you must have seen how the hero (or the detective) takes up a case which nobody else is able to solve. All he does is to break it into pieces. Then decision making becomes easy and he can make progress towards the final solution.

When you don't do this, the enormity of the problem freezes you and you either avoid making any decision, or postpone the decision. Both of these can turn out to be costly mistakes.

A few years back, the entire world was abuzz with the twenty-twenty cricket matches. There were talks about big corporate companies sponsoring cricket teams and making money out of it. This was a new concept. Traditionally, cricket teams were owned by countries or state cricket boards. A private company owning a cricket team, and profiting from it is a very complex scenario indeed.

A few companies took the initiative and started breaking the problem into many smaller questions: How much will it cost me to own a team? What are the indirect costs? How much money can I make out of it? Are there any other benefits in business? If yes, how much? What is the worst that can happen?

You're right; it's the classic 'six thinking hats' thinking. It is now used to break the bigger problem into many smaller ones to analyse them. The same technique has helped those companies to arrive at a conclusion. So they went ahead and bought their respective cricket teams.

At the same time, there were many other companies who were not able to decide if this is a good idea. They were worried about the complexity of the problem, delayed their decision, and lost the opportunity to buy a team.

A couple of years down the line, the companies who bought those teams made enormous profits and are making tons of money. Those who delayed making a decision are now running behind the cricket board for another chance. They may get another chance, that's not the point here. But the original complex problem was something which froze them, and the opportunity was lost. This is a trap which we should avoid.

Once again, think of how you solve a mathematical problem. However complex it may be, you have a process which you follow step-by-step, and you will arrive at the answer sooner or later. Decision making can also be split into a series of steps. We have already seen ten such steps—processes like PM Analysis, Six thinking hats, 80:20 analysis etc. Keep these useful tips in your mind and face your problems confidently.

You need to remember one thing—while making a decision, there are some factors we can control, and some we can't. When we go out to eat, we can control what kind of restaurant we can go to. But we can't really predict how the weather is going to be. If you plan to have an ice cream, and it rains heavily, it spoils your mood for ice cream. We can hardly do anything about it.

It is important to realise what we can control and what is not in our hands. We need to focus on what we can change, and it gives us better chances of winning. At the same time, don't get into the other trap – imagining that nothing can be changed by you. Do a careful analysis of what is around you and make a decision on what you can bring into effect and what you can't. Then focus on those things which you can directly make an impact, and you will realise that success is just round the corner.

Decision making is very important in life. No one can avoid making decisions, whether they are simple ones or drastic ones that can change one's life. So make it as natural as possible. Instead of remembering all the formulas, try embedding it into your thought process and go ahead with the process of decision making.

Over a period of time, it will become as regular as your breathing, and you never have to fear to make a decision.

Good luck to you on all the decisions you are going to make from now on!

Prodigy books

Biographies

Abdul Kalam
Charles Darwin
Marie Curie
Visvesvaraya
Srinivasa Ramanujan
Newton
Einstein
James Watt
Jagadish Chandra Bose
Alexander Graham Bell
Edison
Gandhi
Jawaharlal Nehru
Abraham Lincoln
Mother Teresa
Nelson Mandela
Florence of Nightingale
Ambedkar
Bhagat Sigh
Tipu Sultan
Rani of Jhansi
Akbar
Shivaji
Bharati
Shakespeare
Rabindranath Tagore

Vivekananda
Martin Luther King
Alexander the Great
Napoleon
Adolf Hitler
Charlie Chaplin
Walt Disney
Bill Gates
Narayana Murthy
Columbus
Hsuan Tsang

Classics Retold

Homer's Iliad
The Odyssey
The Tempest
Hamlet
The Merchant of Venice
Twelfth Night
Romeo and Juliet
Macbeth
Hamlet
King Lear
Midsummer Nights Dream
The Ramayana
The Mahabharatha

Other Titles

The Universe
Hinduism
Global Warming
The New 7 wonders of the World
Life
Tsunami
Dinosaurs
Ganga
World War II
Mughals
Planet Earth
Indian History
I - Sultans to Sepoy Mutiny
Madras - Chennai
Exam Tips
Television
Effective Communication
Creative Thinking
Decision Making